Jackson
  County
    Library
      System

HEADQUARTERS:

413 W. Main

Medford, Oregon   97501

THE FIRST VOYAGE
AROUND THE WORLD

Roger Coote

Illustrated by Tony Smith

The Bookwright Press
New York · 1990

Great Journeys

First published in the
United States in 1990 by
The Bookwright Press
387 Park Avenue South
New York, NY 10016

First published in 1989 by
Wayland (Publishers) Limited
61 Western Road, Hove
East Sussex, BN3 1JD, England

Library of Congress Cataloging-in-Publication Data
Coote, Roger.
    The first voyage around the world/by Roger Coote.
        p.   cm. — (Great journeys)
    Bibliography: p.
    Includes index.
    Summary: An account of Ferdinand Magellan's circumnavigation of
the world in the early 1500s.
    ISBN 0–531–18302–5
    1. Magalhães, Fernão de, d. 1521 – Journeys – Juvenile literature.
2. Voyages around the world – Juvenile literature.   [1. Magellan,
Ferdinand, d. 1521. 2. Explorers. 3. Voyages around the world.]
I. Title.   II. Series.
G420.M2C66   1990
910′.92–dc20
[92]
                                                              89–7236
                                                              CIP
                                                              AC

Typeset by DP Press Ltd, Sevenoaks
Printed in Italy by G. Canale & C.S.p.A., Turin

Frontispiece *Ferdinand Magellan (1480–1521)*.

Cover *The* Victoria *was the first ship to circumnavigate the globe. Its journey was through unknown and uncharted waters.*

Contents

The Young Magellan

On September 20, 1520, five ships and 277 men set sail on what was to become one of the greatest journeys in history – the first voyage around the world. The captain of that small fleet was a brilliant Portuguese seaman called Ferdinand Magellan.

Magellan was born around 1480. At the age of twelve, he went to train as a page at the court of Leonor, the Portuguese Queen. He studied music, dancing, hunting and swordsmanship. Because King John II was interested in exploration and trade with other countries, Portuguese pages were also taught astronomy, navigation and map-making. The pages were supervised by the king's brother-in-law, Duke Manuel, who seems to have taken a dislike to young Ferdinand. However, he enjoyed his time as a page, although he longed for the day when he could go to sea.

In 1495 Magellan's hopes seemed to vanish. John II was killed, and Manuel became king. Manuel did not completely share John's interest in the sea and foreign trade. At first he allowed a few expeditions to sail, but Magellan could not gain a place on any of them. Instead he had to help prepare the ships for their voyages, only to see them return to the port of Lisbon crammed with spices, silks, gold and other treasures.

MANVEL·I

Left King John II of Portugal (1455–95). During his reign Bartholomew Diaz became the first European to sail around the Cape of Good Hope.

Below The port of Lisbon in 1550. Portuguese sailors set out from here on their voyages of discovery.

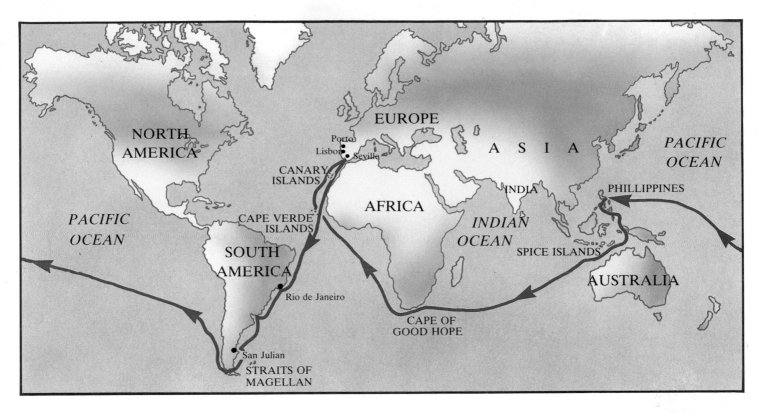

NORTH
AMERICA

EUROPE

Porto
Lisbon
Seville

CANARY
ISLANDS

CAPE VERDE
ISLANDS

PACIFIC
OCEAN

SOUTH
AMERICA

Rio de Janeiro

San Julian
STRAITS OF
MAGELLAN

AFRICA

A S I A

INDIA

INDIAN
OCEAN

CAPE OF
GOOD HOPE

SPICE ISLANDS

PHILLIPPINES

PACIFIC
OCEAN

AUSTRALIA

However, his chance came at last. In 1505 he sailed with a military expedition to India. For the next seven years Magellan worked hard and fought bravely. He was quickly promoted and became an experienced sea captain, visiting the west coast of Africa, India, Malaya and the Moluccas, or Spice Islands. He was also the first European to visit the Philippines. He returned to Portugal in 1512, and a year later went to fight against the Moors in Morocco. He was badly wounded in the knee, and was left with a limp for the rest of his life. To make matters worse, Magellan was accused of stealing some of the booty captured in battle. Although the charge was dropped, Manuel turned against him. Desperate to gain command of a ship, Magellan approached the king directly. His request was refused and he was told that there was no place for him in the Portuguese fleet.

Humiliated, Magellan left Lisbon for Oporto in the north of Portugal. There he worked out a plan to reach the Philippines and the Spice Islands by sailing west rather than east. But how could he sail around the Americas and into the Pacific Ocean? This question was answered by an old friend of Magellan's, John of Lisbon. He believed he had discovered a strait leading from the Atlantic to the Pacific, but had not sailed all the way through it. Magellan's mind was made up. If King Manuel did not want his services, perhaps Charles I of Spain would be interested in his proposal. In October 1517 Magellan left Portugal for Spain. He was never to return.

Above *The route of the first circumnavigation of the world, 1519–22.*

New Worlds

Left This illustration from a map drawn in 1375 shows Marco Polo and his son traveling by camel caravan in Asia.

In 1517, far less was known about the world than is known today. Most people knew that the Earth was round, but they thought it was much smaller than it really is. There were whole continents, such as Australia, that were totally unknown to Europeans. Other faraway countries were known about, but had never been reached by sea.

Between 1271 and 1295 the Venetian traveler Marco Polo had made his way overland to India, China and Japan. From 1420 to 1460, Prince Henry the Navigator sent out ships from Portugal to sail down the west coast of Africa. Then in 1487, during the reign of John II of Portugal, Bartholomew Diaz rounded the southern tip of Africa and sailed into the Indian

Left Prince Henry the Navigator (1394–1460). He founded a school of navigation and map-making, and devoted his life to encouraging Portuguese exploration.

Ocean. Five years later, Christopher Columbus sailed westward from Spain and became the first European to reach the Americas. He thought he had found a route to the

Indies and the Spice Islands, and the Portuguese became extremely jealous of Spain's good fortune. There was fierce rivalry between the two countries, and war was prevented only by the Treaty of Tordesillas in 1494, which divided the world in two. Africa, India, Indonesia and the tip of Brazil were given to Portugal; the rest of the Americas and the Pacific belonged to Spain. No one was sure who controlled the Spice Islands, because no one knew exactly where they were.

Gradually it became clear that Columbus had not reached the Indies. The Portuguese realized that to find their own route to the Spice Islands they would have to sail eastward. In 1497, during one of the few voyages permitted by King Manuel of Portugal, Vasco da Gama sailed around the tip of Africa and reached India. He returned in triumph, with a cargo of fabulous treasures. During the next few years, the Portuguese set up a huge trading empire in the East. Portugal, which had been a poor country, became one of the richest and most powerful countries in Europe.

The most important trade was in spices, especially pepper. This was used throughout Europe to preserve meat and to flavor it when it started to go bad. For centuries, spices had been brought to Europe from the Far East. The journey was long, dangerous and expensive. Many cargoes were lost to pirates and other robbers along the route. By the time the spices reached

Europe, they cost a hundred times more than they had in the East. So a sea route to the Spice Islands was very profitable indeed, as Portugal had discovered. Spain needed to find its own route. The Treaty of Tordesillas meant that Spanish ships would have to sail westward. When Ferdinand Magellan moved from Portugal to Spain, he was given a very warm welcome.

Above left *Christopher Columbus (c1451–1506).*

Above right *Vasco da Gama (c1469–1524).*

Below *This map, drawn in 1558, shows the Spice Islands, or Moluccas.*

Final Preparations

By the end of 1517, Magellan had found three influential men who were willing to give him money for his expedition. They were Juan de Aranda, Bishop Fonseca and Cristobal de Haro. Magellan wanted to explore the Philippines as well as to claim the Spice Islands for Spain. But his financiers were only interested in finding a route to the Spice Islands and making a handsome profit.

Magellan then presented his plan to Charles I. Without the king's approval, no expedition could sail. At first, Charles was rather doubtful, but he was quickly won over and soon agreed to the voyage. This was partly because he was anxious to capture some of the spice trade. Like Magellan, the king was also interested in the Philippines, and he wanted the expedition to claim the islands for Spain. He appointed Magellan Captain General of the expedition. His orders were to sail to the Spice Islands and then on to the Philippines.

As Magellan began to prepare for the voyage, he soon discovered that he had enemies. King Manuel of Portugal sent agents to try to stop the fleet from sailing and to steal the expedition's supplies. Meanwhile, the three Spanish financiers attempted to reduce Magellan's authority. They tried, without success, to persuade Charles to change

Above *A Spanish gold coin showing the coat of arms of Charles I.*

Left *Magellan using navigational equipment.*

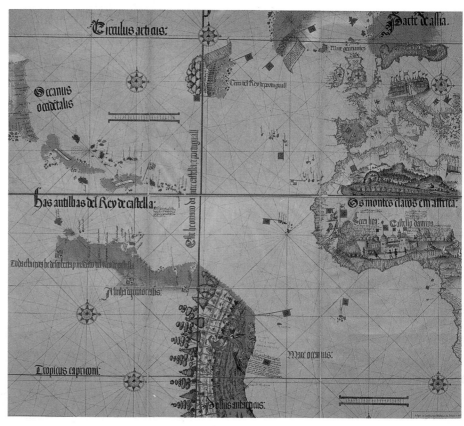

Magellan's orders. They also chose their own men to captain three of the five ships of the fleet, and appointed people sympathetic to their aims to other important positions on the expedition. By the time the fleet was fully manned, Magellan could not count on the loyalty of almost one third of the seamen.

By the end of May 1519, the crews were ready but the stores had not been loaded. Since the voyage would last two years at least, a huge amount of food was needed. Almost 100 tons of ship's biscuits were taken on board, together with nearly 33 tons of salted beef and 26 tons of salted pork. Cheese, dried beans, onions, rice and flour were also loaded, as well as water and wine. Lumber, nails,

canvas and tar were stowed in the ships' holds so that repairs could be carried out. Maps and navigational instruments were taken aboard, along with a huge quantity of weapons to help protect the fleet from Portuguese attackers. Then came the cargo, which included copper bars and bracelets, knives, scissors, mirrors, imitation jewels, fishhooks and colored cloth. The three financiers knew that these would be popular with the spice merchants in the Spice Islands and very saleable.

Finally everything was ready and on September 20, 1519, the fleet sailed out of the harbor at San Lucar de Barrameda and headed into the Atlantic. The voyage had finally begun.

Above *Provisions were loaded aboard the ships in preparation for Magellan's voyage.*

Far left *This map, drawn in 1502, shows how much of the Americas was still unexplored.*

Under Sail

Magellan's five ships were the *Trinidad*, his flagship, the *San Antonio*, *Concepcion* and *Victoria*, captained by the Spanish captains Cartagena, Quesada and Mendoza, and finally the tiny *Santiago*. Not much is known about these ships. They were probably an early type of galleon, with three masts, square sails and a raised deck at the bow and stern.

The first few days of the voyage passed quietly. But when the fleet reached Tenerife, Magellan found out that the Spanish captains were planning to murder him. Sure enough, they tried to cause a quarrel with Magellan. They hoped that a fight would break out during which they could kill him. But Magellan kept his head and bided his time, refusing to be provoked. Some weeks later, when the Spaniards tried once more to seize command, Magellan was ready for them. Cartagena went too far and threatened mutiny. This gave Magellan the excuse he needed, and he had him locked up.

As they sailed south toward the Equator, the ships encountered bad weather. For two weeks they were battered by violent thunderstorms. These electric storms caused a strange effect called St. Elmo's Fire. The ships' masts and rigging glowed with a bright, flickering light. The sailors believed this was a sign that they were being protected by St. Elmo, the patron saint of seamen. Antonio Pigafetta, an Italian who kept a record of the voyage, wrote in his diary: "the saint appeared in the guise of a lighted torch at the head of the mainmast; here he remained for more than two hours, a great comfort to us all."

As it approached the Equator, the tiny fleet was pounded by terrible thunderstorms and huge waves.

After being lashed by high winds and torrential rain, the ships entered the doldrums, a belt of calm water situated along the Equator. With no wind to fill their sails, they stayed almost motionless in the flat, calm sea while the sun beat down on them. The fierce heat melted the tar between the timbers and the ships began to leak. Food went rotten, and the water and wine barrels burst open. Gradually the ocean currents carried them out of the doldrums, and after three weeks they picked up the wind again and set sail for Brazil.

On December 13, 1519, the fleet dropped anchor in one of the most beautiful harbors in the world, Rio de Janeiro. The damage done to the ships during the earlier storms was repaired, and fresh food and water were taken on board. The local Guarani Indians were very friendly, and Magellan's men spent two enjoyable weeks there. When the five ships set out again on Christmas Day, the Guarani followed them, begging them to return.

The Search for El Paso

During the last few days of 1519 the ships sailed down the South American coast. The wind and currents were favorable, and the fleet made good progress. With fresh food and water in the ships' holds, the sailors were content. Magellan was also in good spirits. He was convinced that he was close to finding *el paso*, John of Lisbon's strait leading to the Pacific.

Magellan was also eager to discover the large land mass that was believed to exist beyond the tip of South America. It was known as *Terra Australis Incognita* or "Unknown Southern Land."

On January 11, 1520, the fleet rounded a headland and entered a broad, open channel. Magellan called his men together. He told them that they were about to enter seas where no Christian had ever sailed. The *Santiago* was sent to explore *el paso* while the other ships headed south in search of *Terra Australis*. When the fleet met up again a few days later there was only bad news. Magellan had not found the unknown continent and, worse still, the *Santiago* had discovered that John of Lisbon's strait was not *paso* at all. It was the mouth of a great river.

This was a terrible blow for Magellan. The whole reason for the voyage seemed to have been destroyed. At first Magellan refused to believe the news. He led the fleet into the channel, and would not turn back even when the water became dangerously shallow. Lowering a longboat over the side, he was rowed westward until the truth was too clear to deny.

Once again Magellan called his men together. The crew was mutinous. The officers tried to persuade Magellan to turn around and sail to the Spice Islands via the known route, traveling eastward. The crew urged him to return to Rio de Janeiro. But Magellan was a brave and decisive man and extremely determined. He would not give in.

He insisted that the fleet sail on, and swore that *el paso* must be only a few miles to the south. This did not please the captains at all, but the ordinary seamen were won over. So, early in February they left the estuary we now call the *Rio de la Plata* and turned south again, into the unknown.

In January 1520,
Magellan was convinced
he had found el paso, but
the "strait" turned out to
be a river estuary.

Mutiny at San Julian

At first the small fleet made good progress. They sailed close to the coast, exploring every bay, inlet and river mouth in the hope that it might be *el paso*. But as they sailed farther south the seas became frighteningly rough and the wind grew to hurricane force. Sometimes it even drove the tiny ships backward. The temperature dropped to below freezing point, and thick ice formed on the ships' rigging. For eight weeks they battled through some of the most dangerous waters in the world. During this time, Magellan always led the way in the *Trinidad*.

Eventually, Magellan realized that his crew was exhausted and could go no farther. He began to search for a sheltered harbor where they could spend the winter. On March 31, 1520, the fleet headed into the bay of San Julian. It was a cold, barren and lonely place, surrounded by bleak gray cliffs – very different from Rio de Janeiro. Magellan ordered his men to begin building huts on the shore. As food was running low, he cut the daily rations. The captains and some of the crew objected. But Magellan would not discuss their complaints, and had some of them arrested.

Below *Espinosa, who was loyal to Magellan, tricked the mutinous Captain Mendoza and killed him.*

Just before midnight on April 1, thirty men from the *Concepcion*, led by Cartagena and Quesada, boarded and captured the *San Antonio*. When day broke, Magellan realized that something was wrong. He sent a small boat from the *Trinidad* to each of the other ships in turn to see which of them remained loyal.

Only the *Santiago* allowed Magellan's men on board. At this point Magellan acted swiftly and boldly. He sent one of his men, Gonzales de Espinosa, to the *Victoria* with a private letter for Captain Mendoza. When they were alone, Espinosa gave Mendoza the letter with one hand and stabbed him to death with the other. At the same moment a group of Magellan's loyal crew swarmed aboard the *Victoria* and captured her. With only the *San Antonio* and the *Concepcion* now under their control, and trapped in the harbor by the rest of the fleet, Cartagena and Quesada panicked. They tried to escape but bungled the attempt. The *San Antonio* was captured and the crew of the *Concepcion* surrendered. The mutiny was over.

The trial of the mutineers lasted five days. Quesada was executed, and Cartagena was marooned on the inhospitable shore of Patagonia. The bodies of Quesada and Mendoza were hung up on gibbets around the bay. This left the rest of men in no doubt that Magellan was in charge of their fleet.

Above *After the trial of the mutineers, Magellan ordered that the bodies of Mendoza and Quesada should be hung up on gibbets around the bay of San Julian.*

Disaster and Discovery

Left Magellan's fleet under full sail in the South Atlantic.

With the mutiny over, there was much work to be done. The loyal members of the crew began building huts in which to sleep and to store supplies. The crewmembers who had taken part in the mutiny had a less pleasant task – careening. The ships were beached at high tide and rolled over onto one side. The mutineers then had to scrape away the barnacles from the hull, replace any rotten timbers and pour on boiling tar to seal the seams. Then the other side was treated in the same way. The men were kept in chains and often worked waist-deep in freezing water.

When the huts were built and the provisions were being removed from the ships, Magellan made a terrible discovery. When the ships were loaded in Lisbon, Portuguese spies had managed to make sure that only half the food stores

Above The sailors had never before seen creatures like seals.

were on board. Magellan set the men to work hunting, trapping and fishing to make up for the lost supplies.

In his diary, Pigafetta described some of the strange creatures he had seen as the fleet sailed south. There were "goslings" that had "black and white feathers over their whole body" and "sea wolves" with "a head like a calf and small round "a head like a calf and small

round ears, large teeth and no legs." We now know these animals as penguins and fur seals, but Magellan's men had never seen anything like them.

One day, when the fleet had been at San Julian for two months, a huge man appeared on the shore. He was almost 2.3 m (7.6 ft) tall. A few days later more "giants" appeared. Gradually Magellan succeeded in making friends with them. Then he attempted to capture two of them to take back to Spain. They escaped and, not surprisingly, the "giants'" friendship quickly turned to feelings of hatred.

In May, Magellan sent the *Santiago* farther south to find new winter quarters. The tiny ship ran into terrifying storms and was wrecked in the estuary of the Santa Cruz river. Two of the survivors made their way to San Julian for help.

The four remaining ships spent the rest of the winter at Santa Cruz. Then on August 23, 1520, they set out again. They sailed south into the icy water of the Antarctic. On October 21, a huge storm blew up and separated the ships. The *Trinidad* and the *Victoria* were able to head for the open sea, but the *San Antonio* and the *Concepcion* were driven into a bay lined with jagged rocks. When the storm subsided after forty-eight hours, Magellan went in search of his two missing ships.

Next morning the crew of the *Trinidad* discovered a deep-water strait running to the west. Then the lookout spotted two sails, and the *San Antonio* and the *Concepcion* came toward them. Their flags were flying and the crew was jumping with joy on the decks. Finally, they had found *el paso*.

Above left *A sixteenth-century map showing the tip of South America and the Magellan Strait.*

Above right *The Santa Cruz river as it is today. Magellan's fleet spent the winter here in 1520.*

Into the Vast Ocean

Even though *el paso* had been found, some of the men still wanted to turn around and sail eastward to the Moluccas. Magellan refused to turn back. But while the fleet was exploring the strait, the men on the *San Antonio* mutinied. They managed to slip away and sail the ship back to Spain. Magellan searched for the *San Antonio* for almost three weeks, as she was carrying a large part of the entire fleet's food. But she seemed to have vanished without trace. Again Magellan ordered his men to begin fishing and hunting for food.

On November 27, 1520, the three remaining ships left the strait and headed out into the open ocean. Magellan called his men together for a service of thanksgiving. He told them that they were about to enter a sea where no ship had ever sailed before, and solemnly named it the *Mar Pacifico*, or "Peaceful Sea." He was sure that in three or four days they would be in the Spice Islands. Using the only navigational instruments he had — an hourglass, a compass and a cross-staff — he led the fleet toward the latitude at which he knew the islands should be.

But Magellan's "sea" was in fact the largest ocean on Earth. As the days and weeks passed the crew became bored and then anxious. Magellan himself realized that his calculations were inaccurate. Food was running low and he reduced the daily ration. But the worst was yet to come. As they sailed under the burning sun of the tropics, the little food they had started to go bad, and the water supplies turned yellow. The men ate anything they could find:

As the days and weeks passed during the voyage across the Pacific, the food ran out. The men were reduced to eating anything they could find or catch.

rats, strips of leather from the rigging, sawdust, and even the maggots that crawled from the rotting provisions. They began to get sick. Their arms and legs ached, their gums turned blue and swelled up, and their skin broke out in horrible sores. Six weeks into their journey across the Pacific the men began to die of scurvy.

In their long voyage across the Pacific, the ships found only two small, uninhabited islands. At the first island, the larders were stocked up with food and fresh water. The men set off again with high hopes. But once more the days ran into weeks,

and the food went bad. On February 13, 1521, they saw another island. But they were swept past it, unable to anchor in the deep water. On March 4, the *Trinidad*'s crew ate the last of their food. Magellan knew that if he did not find land within two days all his men would be dead.

By March 6, they had been at sea for ninety-eight days. That morning the lookout clambered up the rigging to his place high among the sails. As he looked to starboard he caught his breath. Twice he opened his mouth but no sound came. Then he cried out, "Praise God! Land! Land!"

Landfall

The land they had reached was one of the Marianas Islands. As the men tried to launch the landing boat, they found themselves surrounded by islanders in canoes. Wielding clubs and spears, they boarded the *Trinidad*. Realizing that the weak, sickly crew was no match for them, they began stealing everything they could carry off. When the islanders refused to return what they had taken, Magellan signaled to his men. Six of the islanders were instantly hit by crossbow bolts.

The others scrambled over the side and paddled back to the shore. Magellan's three ships attacked the village with cannon fire. A landing party went ashore to seize as much food and water as they could carry before the fleet sailed.

On March 16, they sighted more land. Although he did not know it, Magellan had finally reached his destination, the Philippines. He landed first on the uninhabited island of Homonhon, where the crew were able to rest, eat and regain

Above *In the Philippines the crewmen traded with the islanders, exchanging knives, scissors and iron for gold and silk.*

their strength before sailing on again. On March 28, they reached an inhabited island. As he listened to the talk of the local people, Magellan realized that he was back in the islands he had visited years before. He knew then that his ship was the first to have traveled all the way around the world.

Magellan made friends with Colombu, the island's raja, or ruler, and converted him and some of the local people to Christianity. The crewmen were happy to trade with the islanders, and many of them gained a small fortune in gold. The sailors became anxious to leave for the Spice Islands, but Magellan ordered them to sail farther into the Philippines. On April 7, the fleet landed at the island of Cebu. The local raja granted permission to trade, and the ships took on silk, pearls, semi-precious stones and gold in exchange for iron, copper, mirrors, scissors and knives. The raja and his people were converted to Christianity,

and Magellan then claimed the Philippines for Spain.

Once again his officers and crew begged Magellan to sail on. They were not interested in converting the islanders, and Cebu's supply of gold had run out. They only wanted to reach the Spice Islands. Magellan had other plans, which were to lead to his downfall.

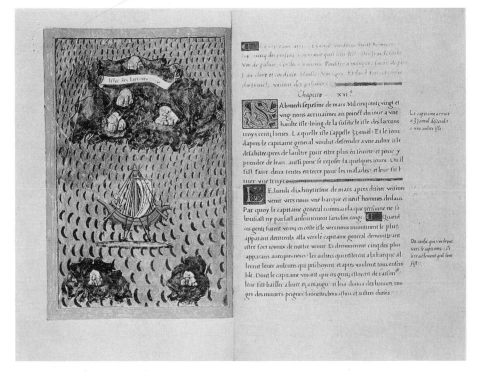

Below This map, from Pigafetta's account of the voyage, shows the Marianas Islands. This was where Magellan's men first went ashore after their long voyage.

Left A fleet of carracks in the early sixteenth century. Ships like these sailed on many Portuguese voyages of exploration.

Tragedy

Magellan's success at converting the Filipinos seems to have made him even more determined to spread Christianity. When the Raja of Cebu told him that the chieftains on some neighboring islands had refused to become Christians, Magellan declared that they would have to be punished. He sent Espinosa with a party of men to attack Cilapulapu, the most powerful of the chieftains. Cilapulapu's island, Mactan, was raided; his soldiers were killed and his capital was burned to the ground. But still the chieftain would not submit.

Magellan was determined to overcome Cilapulapu, despite the protests of his men. He announced that he would lead another attack on Mactan and called for volunteers to go with him. Not one of his Spanish officers offered to help him.

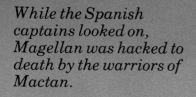

While the Spanish captains looked on, Magellan was hacked to death by the warriors of Mactan.

Raja Colombu offered to send a thousand of his warriors, but Magellan refused. He was convinced that God would lead him to victory.

The landing party consisted of about sixty seamen, stewards and servants. At midnight on April 26, they set off in row boats to launch a surprise attack. It was several hours before the tides allowed them to land. As they waded ashore, cold and wet, they were confronted by 3,000 islanders. Magellan ordered his men to attack, and they began firing their crossbows. They struggled across a series of ditches that Cilapulapu had dug to slow them down. As they moved forward, Magellan saw that they were being lured away from their boats and into a trap. He began to retreat, but as his men went back across the ditches they panicked and ran for the boats. The sailors fought among themselves to get back onto the boats. Magellan and less than a dozen others were left behind.

For almost an hour this small group of men held back the attacking islanders. None of the sailors on board Magellan's ships came to help. Raja Colombu pleaded with the officers, but still they would not go to rescue Magellan. Then the raja launched two of his canoes to pick up the survivors. At last the cannons aboard the *Concepcion* were loaded. But instead of being aimed at Cilapulapu's warriors, they were fired at the raja's canoes. Magellan's last hope was destroyed. He was overpowered and stabbed to death.

This was what the Spanish officers had been waiting for. They immediately sent boats to rescue the four remaining survivors. No effort was made to recover Magellan's body.

Chaos and Treachery

Now that Magellan was dead, the fleet had lost its only capable leader. The Spanish officers tried to negotiate with Colombu, Cilapulapu and the Raja of Cebu all at the same time. The rajas seemed willing to forgive and forget. They invited the officers ashore for a lavish banquet. When most of the Spaniards were thoroughly drunk, the Raja of Cebu gave a signal. Immediately the officers were attacked, and nearly all were killed. Espinosa and John Carvalho had sensed a trap and had managed to escape in time.

It was Carvalho who now took charge of the fleet. His first act was to sink the *Concepcion*. There were only 115 men left out of the 277 who had set out

Above *The Spanish officers were lured ashore for a banquet. At a given signal, the islanders attacked and killed almost all of them.*

from Spain – not enough to sail all three ships. But before he set fire to the *Concepcion*, Carvalho loaded on board her all of Magellan's papers. These included his log books, diary and charts, and even his personal letters. Carvalho hoped to destroy all evidence of his own deceit and treachery.

The *Trinidad* and the *Victoria* then put to sea. The following day they spotted a trading junk on its way to China. The junk was boarded, her crew massacred and the cargo of spices was captured. The Spaniards had become no better than pirates. They then embarked on a four-month campaign of thieving and murder. The two ships sailed the southwest Pacific, attacking unarmed trading vessels and ports. Arguments and fights broke out among the Spaniards. Carvalho was deposed and

Espinosa took command. He put an end to the piracy and began to search for the Spice Islands. At every island he reached, Espinosa asked for directions to the Moluccas. Eventually on November 8, 1521, the islands came into view.

The men landed on the island of Tidore and were warmly welcomed. The King of Tidore invited them to live and trade on the island. They presented the king with gifts and spent three pleasant months there, resting and trading. The sailors even helped to build a fort to guard the harbor entrance. But at the beginning of 1522 Espinosa and his men began to prepare for their return journey. They cleaned out the ships' bilges, mended the sails and loaded up with fresh food and water. Then they filled the holds with the cargo they would carry home to Spain.

Below Carvalho and his men took to piracy. They attacked any trading ship they came across, stole its cargo and killed the crew.

The Homeward Journey

Huge amounts of cloves, pepper, nutmeg and sandalwood were loaded, along with gold, silk, porcelain and precious jewels. In fact the *Trinidad's* cargo was so heavy that she sprang a leak. Espinosa ordered half of his men to set sail for Spain in the *Victoria*. The other half would stay behind to repair the *Trinidad*. They drew lots to decide who would go. On February 21, 1522, the *Victoria* set off with sixty men on board, commanded by Sebastián del Cano. Ahead of them was a long and hazardous journey.

Espinosa remained behind with the rest of the men. When the *Trinidad* was repaired, they sailed out into the Pacific. Before long, the ship was captured by a Portuguese fleet, and most of Espinosa's men were hanged as pirates.

Meanwhile, del Cano was doing his best to avoid a similar fate. He knew that all of the ports between Timor and Europe were controlled by the Spaniards' enemies, the Portuguese. He also knew that he and his few men would not be able to fight off an attacking Portuguese ship. But he was determined to reach Spain. When the tropical heat turned the food rotten and scurvy set in once more, the men begged del Cano to head for the east coast of Africa and surrender to the Portuguese. He refused, just as Magellan would have done.

Above *In May 1522, del Cano and his men sailed around the Cape of Good Hope at the southern tip of Africa.*

Even though he had been one of the mutineers at San Julian, del Cano now seemed to take on the strength of the leader he had tried to depose.

On May 16, the *Victoria* rounded the Cape of Good Hope. Slowly the ship sailed up the west coast of Africa but still could not put into port. Men were dying all the time. When the ship reached the Cape Verde Islands on July 8, only twenty-four men were still alive. All the water and food were gone, and del Cano knew he had to risk going ashore. At midnight he landed on a quiet beach with some of his men. The local fishermen gave them rice and water. But when Portuguese soldiers arrived, del Cano was forced to flee and leave some of his men behind.

The *Victoria* sailed on. Finally, on September 6, 1522, she dropped anchor in the Bay of San Lucar in southern Spain almost three years after she had left. Of the 277 men who had sailed with Magellan's small fleet, only eighteen had survived. They were the first men to sail around the world in a single voyage.

Above The tiny *Victoria*, the first ship to sail around the world.

Left A village in the Cape Verde Islands today. On the return journey, del Cano landed on one of the islands to try to get food for his starving men.

Magellan's Legacy

Magellan's voyage was perhaps the greatest feat of exploration ever accomplished. The journey was a remarkable example of seamanship, and as such, will never be surpassed. In circumnavigating the globe, the *Victoria* traveled more than 67,500 km (42,000 mi). Over 35,000 km (21,800 mi) were through waters never before sailed by Europeans. It was Magellan who had led his men through these uncharted seas.

Magellan added greatly to the geographical knowledge of the world at the time. He proved that it was possible to sail around the southern tip of South America. He also showed beyond any doubt that the world was round and that it was much larger than anyone had previously believed.

In the fifty years after his death, a number of ships tried to follow his route through *el paso*. They all failed. Some people came to believe that Magellan's Strait had simply disappeared. Then in 1578 Francis Drake sailed around the tip of South

Below *This map shows the route taken by Magellan and del Cano on the first voyage around the world.*

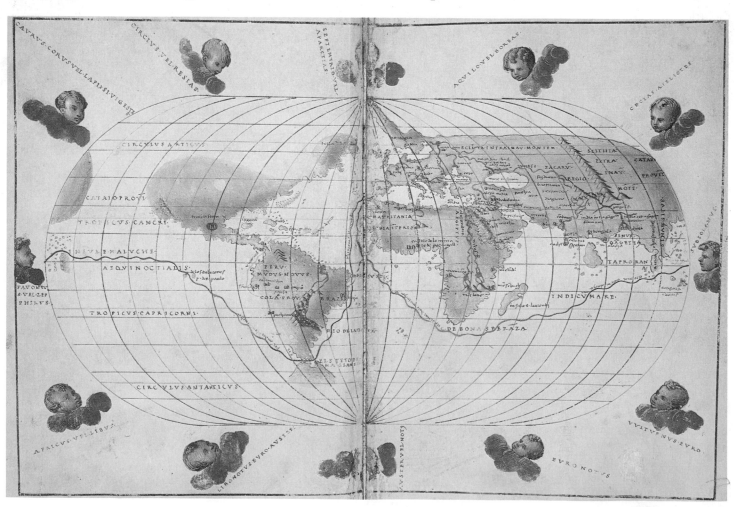

Above *Francis Drake (1540–96), who sailed around the world in 1577–80.*

Above *Ferdinand Magellan, the greatest seaman of his time. In spite of his remarkable achievement, we would know almost nothing about him if it were not for Pigafetta's account of the voyage.*

America during his own voyage around the world. He was the first European after Magellan to enter the Pacific.

In spite of Magellan's great achievements, we do not know very much about him. Not surprisingly, the Portuguese regarded him as a traitor to his own country. Then, when the crew of the *San Antonio* returned to Spain after their mutiny, they did all they could to blacken Magellan's name. All of Magellan's papers and almost all of the true records of the voyage had been destroyed. In fact, Magellan might have been forgotten but for Pigafetta and his diary.

Apart from the treachery of his men, there is another reason why Magellan's name was not well known. He had set out to discover a short westward route to the Spice Islands. This would have helped Spain seize some of the Portuguese spice trade and would have brought Spain enormous wealth. But the lands he found were far away. The route was so hazardous that it was never used. Eventually, after years of argument, it was shown that the Philippines were not even in Spain's half of the world. They lay on the Portuguese side of the line that had been agreed earlier in the Treaty of Tordesillas.

Glossary

Barnacles Hard-shelled creatures that attach themselves to the underneath of ships.

Bilge The lowest part of the inside of a ship, where dirty water and rubbish collects.

Bolt An arrow fired from a crossbow.

Booty Valuable objects captured from an enemy in battle.

Careen To push a ship over on one side to clean or repair it.

Circumnavigate To sail or fly all the way around the world.

Compass An instrument for finding direction. It has a magnetized needle that swings to point toward the magnetic north pole.

Conversion A change in a person's religious beliefs.

Cross-staff, or astrolobe. An instrument for measuring latitude using the position of the stars.

Doldrums A belt of light winds and calm seas in the region of the Equator.

Equator An imaginary line around the middle of the Earth, halfway between the North and South Poles.

Filipino Someone who was born or lives in the Philippines.

Financier Someone who provides money for a project, such as an expedition.

Galleon A type of ship used for both trade and warfare from about the fifteenth to the eighteenth century.

Gibbet A wooden structure on which the bodies of executed criminals were hung on display.

Hold The area inside a ship where cargo is stored.

Hourglass An instrument for measuring time. Sand runs from an upper container to a lower one through a narrow opening, taking exactly one hour.

Junk A flat-bottomed sailing vessel used in the waters around China.

Latitude The distance of something from the Equator, measured in degrees. 0° is the Equator, 90°N is the North Pole and 90°S is the South Pole.

Log book The daily record of a ship's voyage, often kept by the captain.

Marooned To be stranded on an island without a safe way to escape.

Moors Muslim people of North Africa, descended partly from Arabs.

Mutiny Rebellion by seamen or soldiers against their officers.

Ration A certain amount of food and drink, which seamen are allowed each day.

Scurvy A disease caused by lack of vitamin C, a vitamin found in fresh fruit and vegetables.

Scuttle To deliberately sink a ship.

Shoal A stretch of shallow water, often over a sandbank or rocky area.

Strait A narrow channel linking two large areas of sea.

Tropics The area of the Earth between latitudes 23½°N and 23½°S. These latitudes are called the Tropic of Cancer and the Tropic of Capricorn.

Finding Out More

The age in which Magellan lived was a very exciting and eventful one. A good way of finding out about the kind of life he lived is to investigate the history of Spain and Portugal during the sixteenth century.

Adventure and exploration is not only found in the history of the Mediterranean. There were many famous, and an even larger number of relatively-unknown explorers living around the world during this period. Your local museum may contain models of the kinds of ships they used, examples of their navigational equipment and the sorts of clothes they wore.

Books to Read

Your local library should be able to help you find these books.

Allan Blackwood, *Ferdinand Magellan*. Bookwright, 1986

W.D. Browlee, *The First Ships Around the World*. Lerner Pubns., 1977

Richard Humble, *The Voyage of Magellan*. Franklin Watts, 1989

Jonathan Rutland, *See Inside a Galleon, Rev. Edn.* Warwick, 1986

Cass Sandak, *Explorers and Discovery*. Franklin Watts, 1983

Gardner Soule, *Christopher Columbus on the Green Sea of Darkness*. Franklin Watts, 1988

Picture Acknowledgments

The publishers would like to thank the following for allowing their illustrations to be reproduced in this book:

Aldus Archive 4 (top), 6 (top), 7 (top left), 8 (bottom), 21 (top), 28; Barnaby's Picture Library 17 (top right), 27 (bottom); Mary Evans 8 (top left), 26; Michael Holford 6 (bottom), 7 (bottom), 17 (top left), 17 (bottom), 21 (bottom); Peter Newark's Historical Pictures 7 (top right), 16 (top), 27 (top), 29 (top left); Photri *frontispiece*, 29 (right); Ronald Sheridan's Ancient Art and Architecture Collection 4 (bottom), 8 (top right); Tony Stone Worldwide 16 (bottom).

Index

Page numbers in *italics* refer to illustrations